NEVERTHELESS

AN EXPRESSION OF OPPRESSION

MONIKA KARIKALAN

ISBN 978-1-63714-321-6

To all those who thrive for a change.

Contents

Preface · vii

Acknowledgements · ix

Prologue · xi

  1. Feminism? Yes · 1

Part 1

  2. Rape · 5

Part 2

  3. Rapist Husbands · 13

Part 3

  4. The Blame · 19

Part 4

  5. Period Shaming · 25

Part 5

  6. Marriage Vs Career · 33

Part 6

  7. Gender Stereotyping · 37

Part 7

  8. Domestic Violence · 45

Part 8

  9. Mass Media · 51

Part 9

  10. Sympathy? No · 57

Part 10

Epilogue · 61

Contents

A Note From A Friend About The Author   63

Preface

Unable to bear the indifferences towards the injustices around me, I was searching for a way to express my insights. The easiest way for this young girl from a small town is writing. I may not be regarded as articulate but I ought to express my insights and intolerance towards the oppressions. I am not the only one who has an impulse to raise voice. Most of us want to. Unfortunately, most of us do not. I just don't want to be one of those, who have an ability to put up with the inequalities.

Edward Bulwer-Lytton once told "The pen is mightier than the sword." I really don't know if it's mightier. But I can say for sure it's **Nevertheless.**

Acknowledgements

Thanks to the inequalities I witnessed in my life. Without you, how could I have thought of writing this book!

A big thanks to **Jasmine M Moosa** for letting us include her tale and to the organisation **Humans of Bombay** for being a medium through which I reached out. This is included with the full knowledge and consent of the former.

A special mention to my proofreader friend Vibra priya. Thank you Aarthi for being my personal motivator. You made the initiation of this book. Thank you my dearest Yazhini for writing such a sweet afterword about me.

I can't thank but give a big hug to all my friends who have been my biggest support. Thank you for believing in me.

Note : The term 'Nevertheless' is used in this book to emphasize the meaning of equality.

Prologue

In this book, you will come to know about the persecutions and oppressions that women face under 10 categories and the reasons behind them. Meanwhile, you will also witness a story of a survivor.

You may find me selfish at some instances of the book. Indeed, I am selfish. I don't want a change that will happen for my great granddaughter. I want a change for me.

You may find me offensive too. But I refuse to apologize. Because every single woman faces at least 3 of these oppressions without even a little hope for justice.

Go ahead. You won't regret.

CHAPTER I

FEMINISM? YES

"If you stand for equality, then you are a Feminist. Sorry to tell you. - Emma Watson"

What comes to your mind, when you come across the word 'Equality'? And what comes to your mind when you come across the word 'Feminism'?

I can say for sure; you people might not have felt good for the latter as you have felt for the former. Infact, Feminism by definition is the movement supporting women's rights on the grounds of *equality* for the sexes. Clearly, both these words are the same by roots. The only reason for emphasizing women's rights is that, in most cases, women are denied their rights.

Most of us are not familiar with the word 'masculinism' which is the advocacy for the rights of men. Why is it so? Apparently, the rights for men are taken for granted. Whereas, women had to struggle on a daily basis to get them.

While the feminists are trying to make changes in the perceptions, there are animals who are hunting women, abusing them and taking their lives away, *inhumanly*. Here, humanity is being questioned. As a consequence, the term 'Feminism' gets a new synonym called 'Humanism'. The priority given to the definition of this well-known word reflects that it is being totally misunderstood. The problem is that this misunderstanding leads to the suppression of the inborn Feminism. Infact, many such feminists are unwilling to admit or present themselves as a feminist. Even Malala Yousufzai once hesitated in saying 'Am I a feminist or not'. I wonder who could be a better feminist than Malala. Gratitude to the UN Women Goodwill Ambassador Emma Watson for her speech at UN headquarters, Newyork, 2014. She has led a new path regarding Feminism.

Let me take you to the grounds of reason behind this misunderstanding before I intend to move further.

PATRIARCHY:

When a person looks over Feminism, wearing sunglasses called Patriarchy, there arises this crisis. Though those glasses may seem cool on that person, only he/she knows whether it is serving them any good or not. Then, this person starts to insist others wear them. If not, they will blame the vision of others. I would never corner men alone for this patriarchal perception. I personally know women who are 100% patriarchal. Women, who consider men as their superior, also come under this circle. These people often come up with a question, 'Are you a Feminist?'. They never wait for the other to answer. Instead, they end up the question with a giggle. What's funny here? Never let anyone's sarcasm stop you speaking out for a good cause. Next time, when you are asked this question, tell them YES before they let out their giggle.

"If NO is indispensable in Feminism, YES is too."

Jasmine belonged to an orthodox Muslim family in Kerala. The place she lived is where girls aren't meant to have a voice. Jasmine's biological father left her mother as soon as Jasmine was born. He left only because of the fact that Jasmine is a girl child. After the remarriage of her mother, she lived with her step- father and siblings. She lived in such a lifestyle where men take all the decisions and women should remain as if they don't even exist. Women served food for men and ate after they had done. They were supposed to do so. Jasmine thought it was normal. She used to go to school and do chores at home.

Her life was normal until one day, when she returned home from school. There were 2 people sitting in the veranda. She served them tea as instructed by her mother. She was still in her school uniform. They smiled at her, when she served them tea. She had no idea what was going on around her. After they left the place, Jasmine was shocked to know from her mother that they had come to see her to get her married to the boy who came. Her mother told her that she is soon to be married.

Jasmine wasn't expecting it. She had also realised that there was something wrong with the boy. She could see the symptoms of autism. She tried to convey this to her mother but her mother denied saying that he was just shy. But Jasmine couldn't take this. She didn't want to get married. She had to refuse for the first time in her life. She said 'No' in a tone she never said before. But there is no one to listen. Her concern was totally neglected and her marriage was fixed. She tried everything she could do to make them understand.

She even stayed hungry. Meanwhile, her mother blackmailed her emotionally with her suicidal threats.

According to her family, calling off the marriage would bring shame to the family and her sisters were yet to be married. Finally, Jasmine decided to call her to-be-husband. But what she got was just disappointment. Instead of listening to her, he asked her, 'what are you wearing right now?' Now, Jasmine had no way out.

Nikah took place without even the presence of the bride. Her father simply handed her over to a man she didn't even know.

CHAPTER II

RAPE

"Rape is one of the most terrible crimes on earth and it happens every few minutes. The problem with the groups who deal with rape is that they try to educate women about how to defend themselves. What really needs to be done is teaching men not to rape. Go to the source and start there. - Kurt Cobain "

What's crueller on earth than a rape. It has become a usual scenario. Isn't it? Flashes of news, 18-year-old girl was raped, 15-year-old girl was raped, 5-year-old child was raped, 6 months old baby was raped and it continues. With the passage of time nothing has changed but the ages of the victims. A girl child can only be safe in her mother's womb until her parents know about her gender. I doubt if the dead bodies can ever be safe. If those aggressors can rape a girl when she is alive, they probably do rape a dead body since the body cannot defend. Ultimately, *a woman can never be safe, regardless of whether she is alive or dead.*

The cases that come into light are frightening and what frightens me more are the cases that have been silenced. The stats broke me into pieces and they were as though yelling at me, 'you should be ashamed of belonging to this human race.' Indeed, I am ashamed. Each and every one should be ashamed. I am ashamed that even while writing this chapter, I could hear the news in my television telecasting the case of Manisha. The stats are such that while I am writing a single word of this book, a girl is being abused. According to the survey conducted by Statista research department (July 27,2020), the number of cases reported in 2018 is over 33,000 with 93% of them committed by someone known to the victim. This shows that a woman is not safe in her own personal environment. The worst part is that only 11% of the cases are ever reported.

The so-called reasons for rape:

1) They shouldn't have let her out late in night.
I defend that, grab the freedom from your son so that he won't be a threat to a girl late at night.
2) Way of dressing.
If you think dressing is the stimulation of rape, if you think there is something wrong in the dress of the victim, think again. What the hell is wrong with the dressing of a 6-month-old baby? When she is in jean, she is raped; When she is in salwar, she is raped; when she is in burqa, she is raped; when she is in *diaper*, she is raped. Obviously, rape has nothing to do with the clothing of the victim but the idiotic mindset of the culprit.
3) Love failure.
If he could rape a girl who he had loved, it isn't love at all. There is no love, it's called lust. In most of the cases, this reason is just brought up to conceal the guiltiness of the culprit and to character assassinate the victim. However, many Indian parents consider love as a crime and this adds to the misery of the victim.

The actual reasons:

1. Gender discrimination
2. Caste system
3. Way of bringing up of the culprit

Gender discrimination:

Indian men, often in the rural regions, have an idea that a woman's duty is doing chores in the household, bringing up their children and serving their in-laws. Then they imagine a perfect woman wrapped up in sari all the time. Some even consider women as reproducing machines. Due to all these misconceptions, when a woman breaks one of these stereotypes, she is stamped as an imperfect woman susceptible to molestation. This mindset is the cause of rape especially in Nirbhaya's case. It was told that those animals who tore her apart, find it inappropriate since she was outside late at night with her male friend. A peculiar thing to note is that her male friend wasn't a threat, but the discriminative mindset of those culprits. Next time, when you discriminate against a girl for her gender jokingly, remember the pain of Nirbhaya when she was dumped in a ditch with her intestines outside her body. Go through the detailed sufferings of her case and you'll never discriminate against a girl.

Caste system:

Both in Asifa and Manisha's cases, the caste system plays the evilest role. These innocent souls had been raped and killed only because of their birth in a lower caste. You can justify the prevalence of the caste system in this 21st century, but this is unacceptable. I just feel like asking everyone who belongs to the so-called upper castes, 'Aren't you ashamed of belonging to that caste?'. Some of you may be proud of the caste you belong to. I could see people every day posting their craziness towards their castes and celebrating leaders not because of their achievements, only because of their caste. Do you people realize what you are doing? Those pride posts are doing nothing butsowing the seeds of rape. Throw away your caste surnames. Throw away those seeds of rape that hung with you all the time. If you can defend that this caste system is meant for the upliftment of the lower castes, before uplifting them, *protect them* from the social animals. Ensure their basic human rights first.

Way of upbringing of the culprit:

Once a rapist was interviewed and was asked what caused him to commit rape. Interestingly, he told a story. He said that when he was young, his mother used to scold his sister for wearing short skirts while going out. Eventually, he got an idea that a girl who dresses minimally, is not a good girl. He justified that he raped a bad girl. From this story, we could easily conclude that there is a problem in the way of parenting itself. If men understand that dressing is in preference to comfort and isn't a big deal, this won't be a problem. *Teach your son that women have a freedom of dressing, instead of teaching your daughter what they should and shouldn't wear.*

JUSTICE?

We just know those cases where the victim is no more. There are still a lot of cases unreported in the media. We remember the names of the victims but not the culprits. From now on let us remember them to ensure that they are ashamed.

Sadly, in our country death penalty is specified only for most extreme cases, which means that the victim should die out of pain to demand justice. Hanging isn't sufficient for such an evil crime. Assault them publicly, whip them off, cut their private parts and then hang them.

"It still can't equate the pain they have caused."

On the night of the wedding, all she could do was run around the bed to get away from him. She screamed and cried helplessly. So, her mother-in-law made her sleep in her room. Next day, her father was called and Jasmine was sent with him. She was glad that she preferred death rather than being forced to bed with a stranger.

The scenario in her house was as she expected. Her mother repeated those suicidal threats. For them, Jasmine had brought shame to the family. But this time, she refused to go back no matter what. She even threatened them to commit suicide so that the shame occurred can be resolved. They asked her not to take any steps until her sisters got married. She didn't want to bother them so She stayed quiet for a year. Her family considered her as a burden and she knew it.

Once their lives were settled, she asked for divorce. Her parents expected this and they couldn't refuse. They realized that they had made a mistake. Subsequently, they were called to sit for the divorce proceedings. Jasmine had to sit in another room while the men discussed her marriage. The patriarchy was so deep that she was not even allowed to sit there to talk about her own life. Her parents told them that they had hidden the fact that the guy had autism. But the villagers started to blame them saying that they should have cross checked. Jasmine could hear them. She remained quiet. Someone said, 'In Islam, if husband asks for sex, wife can't say 'no'. If she does, she is the lowest of the low'. Jasmine couldn't take this anymore. For everyone's astonishment, she came out and confronted the man who came there to represent her husband. She asked him what he would have *done if his daughter was in her place. Everyone was shocked since they didn't expect a girl to speak up.*

Since Jasmine refused to give up, they finalized the divorce. She found her freedom again with the three words 'talaq, talaq, talaq' written on a piece of paper.

But her freedom didn't live long.

CHAPTER III

RAPIST HUSBANDS

"I say nothing, not one word, from beginning to end, and neither does he. If it were lawful for a woman to hate her husband, I would hate him as a rapist — Philippa Gregory, <u>The Red Queen</u> "

'Marital rape', the term we hardly perceive in our entire lifetime. However, this *crime* occurs often covertly. Let me explain the meaning of this term first and then the reason for the concealment of such an issue.

Marital rape is the rape committed by a person with whom the victim is married. When a woman is bound by an agreement called marriage, her consent in terms of sexual relationship is often completely neglected. This is the case in most of the Indian arranged marriages. I am not trying to condemn the arranged marriage system. My point is that this system is the major reason for many women being indifferent to such a crime. Though, marital rape is legal in India, this is undoubtably a legalized crime.

Reasons

1. Family honours prevent a woman from expressing her likes and dislikes regarding her physical relationship with her spouse. They act as if, no such thing ever happens.
2. Lack of awareness among the women.

3. Women are not given the right to take her own decisions over her body.
4. Cultural norms and religious beliefs say that a woman should obey her husband even if her consent is disobeyed.
5. Indian judiciary system argues that proposing marital rape as illegal will lead to anarchy in families since our country upholds family values. Here, culture is prioritized over consent.
6. Patriarchal overview which treats women as if they are emotionless sexual objects.
7. Mindset of a few men out there, who think that they don't need to ask women for consent.
8. Mindset of few religiously bound women. They see their husbands as their superior and they never dare to speak out.
9. Lack of sex education. Considering the topic, a taboo is the major drawback.

I made a quick experiment, asking my Instagram followers about marital rape. I got a few unexpected responses. My female friends had no idea about marital rape but they asked me to explain. Some of my male friends, on the contrary, knew about it. They came up with the terms like 'legalized crime' and 'non-criminalized crime'. After the responses to the story I had posted, two totally different conversations were initiated. One told that there is no solution for this problem since a woman cannot act against her husband who she depends upon. Another told a solution exactly as I had in my mind. The solution that person told me was: A woman should be literate and financially independent. So that she could divorce her rapist husband if needed. That's the perfect solution. Isn't it?

From whom do you expect the solution to come from? A man or a woman?

That was a gentleman. And that was a woman friend who told me there was no solution. Thanks to both. The problem is apparently in the mindset of a few women like her too. The biggest fear about society is a major hurdle while overcoming this problem.

A note to women:

Dear women,

We can't wait for ages to come up with a judicial backup. You need not worry about your family honours if those honours don't honour your consent. If your religion doesn't worry about your emotions, you need not worry about your religion. If your culture grabs your self-respect, what is the use of beholding that culture. These laws are just meant to protect the raping husbands from their guiltiness. You have a voice and soul. Speak out your wells and wishes as well your dislikes. Don't ever hesitate to tell what you feel. Maybe your man is ready to accept your NO. But the question is 'Are you ready to utter your NO?'. He has no rights to force you. Remember, if he forces, he is nothing less than a rapist.

A note to men:

Dear men,

Your girl isn't an object. She has insights and moods. She has feelings like you and me. Yes, she loves you. Yet, she will love you more if you ask for her consent. She may say yes or no. She need not justify her NO. Remember, if you are not willing to accept her NO, you are a rapist too.

"Rape is Rape"

Each day felt like a battle. She wasn't allowed to complete her education. Jasmine was self-sufficient though. She wanted to work. Every single day, she would say, 'I want to work' like a mantra. After so much of struggling, they let her work. They had no other choice.

She applied and got a job as an executive at a vehicle showroom. Though Jasmine used to be meek, she had to speak and convince the customers to buy scooters. This had boosted her self-confidence not only in her work place but also at her home. But the society is never meek. It always reminded her that she was a divorcee.

People would stare at her on the bus, whisper behind her back. Some even taunted her at her face saying, 'oh, he divorced you!'. Initially, she felt ashamed. She used to hide from anyone she knew. But then, she asked herself 'why should I hide?'. She then began to say, 'He didn't divorce me. I divorced him!'. Eventually, the pressure started to mount at home. 'when will you get married?'- the question roared. Her family would send people to see her at her office without even informing her. It was the same drama in a loop.

Jasmine accepted the idea of marriage with one condition. She insisted on talking to the guy before she said yes. She began meeting guys but either she rejected them or she was rejected for being straight forward. She told her past to each guy without shame. This continued for a while until one day, a well-built guy came to see her.

CHAPTER IV

THE BLAME

"We must send a message across the world that there is no disgrace in being a survivor of sexual violence. The shame is on the aggressor - Angelina Jolie "

After reading the previous chapters on Rape and Marital rape, you people may get an idea about the pain of several women during such a bad time. The victim's suffering does not end here. It extends with the inclusion of societal concerns. The society influences the crisis by *blaming and shaming* the victim, instead of standing against the culprit. The worst-case scenario is when the victim's family itself stands against the victim. This further increases the mental trauma of the victim. She struggles to resume an ordinary life. She acquires an injury in her confidence.

Cases have been reported where the victim's family itself punish or even *murder* the victim for the shame occurred and, in some cases, they even disguised it as a suicide. This is worse than the rape itself. The rapist might be someone unknown or someone who doesn't care for the welfare of the victim. But how could you justify the killing of your own daughter. If they think, getting raped is shameful, then what about raping. Why don't those parents of the rapists kill their sons for such a shameful crime? The answer for this interrogation is very simple. The rapist is a man and the victim is a woman (in most cases). The hidden conscience that is hindered from being spoken out is that men are often forgiven for their crimes. The ridiculous thing about this is that women are often unforgiven for the crimes,*they never committed*. The consideration of getting raped as a humiliation is nothing but another form of patriarchy.

Considering the topics regarding sexual violence as a 'taboo' is indirectly a reason for the consideration of getting raped as a 'shame'. The assumption of rape as a taboo in the Indian society can be reflected by a simple example i.e., Most of the parents hesitate to discuss the news with regard to sexual assaults with their children. They even change the TV channels whenever the rape cases are telecasted. This definitely creates an impact especially in the mindset of children under the age of 18. They perceive this topic as a taboo and never get an opportunity to differentiate between good and bad. What they perceive at a young age will stay within for a long time. Thus, it is a parent's responsibility to teach their kid to hate such a crime as rape and the rapists involved and to stand for the justice of the victims.

The survivor

Talking about sexual assaults, it's indeed a duty and an honour to write about a super-woman. This inspiring lady who runs an NGO 'Prajwala' against trafficking of women into sexual exploitation, was gang raped by eight men at the age of 15. She has rescued many girls and children from sex trafficking. She has scripted 14 documentary films on social issues. She published 4 books on anti-trafficking and HIV survival. She has won several awards. She is Sunitha Krishnan. Believe me, being a survivor of rape isn't a shame. She is a warrior and her battle was not an easy one.

"Family honours are not meant to be kept in the vaginas. "

Jasmine told him the truth when she spoke to him. He seemed to be broad-minded. Infact, when she told him that she was still virgin, he said that it didn't matter. She felt it was unbelievable. She liked him and agreed to marry him. She happily attended her nikah.

On the night of the wedding, she was waiting for him. She was full of anticipation. He entered the room and before she could even react, he slapped her and she fell on the floor. Jasmine couldn't understand what had just happened. She gathered all her courage and asked him why he had slapped her.

He pulled her hair and asked, 'what else do you expect? You're second-hand.'

CHAPTER V

PERIOD SHAMING

"Menstruation is not a problem, poor menstrual hygiene is — Anurag Chauhan "

For men who don't know about periods: *Periods* is a natural biological phenomenon that occurs every month between puberty and menopause. Women bleed for three or more days and the physiological changes differ for each individual.

I am not in a spirit to give a definition of periods because I personally believe that every man should be aware of menstruation since it is a usual process just like other natural phenomena like digestion and respiration. The only difference is that it happens only for women, transmen and a few nonbinary or genderqueer people.

Period shaming can be stated as discrimination against women on accounts of menstruation. When a woman is humiliated for her bleeding vagina, it comes under period shaming. In simple words, *periods shaming is nothing but what an average Indian woman faces every month.*

Women are being embarrassed just because they are on their periods. They have to deal with this mainly due to the superstitions that are being followed in our country for no reason. Considering a woman in her periods as impure is still prevailing in India especially in the rural areas. Women in periods are prohibited from entering temples. This inhuman discrimination exists within the houses too. Women are asked not to enter the living room, kitchen and not to touch any utensil or cloth. They are even forced to sit in one corner of the house. They are literally abandoned within their own house. No one will touch them during periods.

Let me elaborate a few incidents that happened and are happening in this democratic country.

1) **Prove that you are not on your periods**: 63 girls in a college were forced to show their underwear to the lady staff to prove that they were not on their periods. This incident took place in Gujarat in a well reputed religious institution. When these girls came forward and reported what they had faced, more shocking information was obtained. The college hostel makes it mandatory that every girl has to register their periods. This is done to track the menstruating girls and they have a set of rules for them like not to go near the temple, not to touch other students and to sit separately in the classroom. When these girls expressed their opposition by not admitting and registering their periods, this inhuman incident took place.

2) **Get out of the house**: In some rural and undeveloped areas, the practice of abandoning women from their houses still prevails. They make it a practice to sleep on the floor in the porch or veranda of the house. The saddest part is that women follow them without questioning, some even believe that is the way to keep their houses pure and divine.

3) **Get out of the village**: The previously mentioned practice is nothing when compared to this. The state which has Manchester Mumbai as its capital, is still blinded by the dark and unhealthy superstitions. A district in Maharashtra called, Gadchiroli has a weird practice that is complete nonsense. Every woman should stay out of the village in a basic hut called gaokar during menstruation. They are banished from entering the village. And this place where

they stay during periods is obviously unsafe. Eventually, they are being abused there.

Reasons behind the problem

- Firstly, the major reason for this problem is some women itself. They are the one who don't want to know the reason behind the cultural customs. Obviously, these were in practice in earlier days when a bleeding woman can attract the attention of an animal. They asked women to sit in a corner just to make sure they don't do any sort of work. They insisted women sleep on the floor just because of the stains. Clearly, menstruation has nothing to do with impurity or agnosticism. This has to be made clear to women.
- Secondly, the reason for literate women to follow this is our subconscious mind. When we do something regularly, we forget to ask a question 'why?'. This practice has been fooling us by making us believe that periods are impure for no obvious reason. So, don't believe anything blindly. Ask for the reason. If there is no answer, refuse to follow them.
- Don't make it too complicated. If God hates women for their pain of bleeding, he shouldn't have given them that pain. If you are not allowed to enter into a temple, stop worshipping that God instead of wasting your precious time in the struggles to change it. We couldn't afford our time in changing all the nonsense around us. It's better to ignore the unworthiness if the change has no use. The level of unworthiness is such that I pity those who oppose the change.

We women are always busy in telling what we want. In the course of time, we forget to tell what we don't. Let me mention some.

- We don't want to be judged by the stain in our cloth.
- We don't want to smuggle the sanitary pads.
- We don't want to replace 'suffering from cramps' with 'suffering from fever'.
- We don't want that feeling of prohibition in the name of God.
- We don't want to be abandoned within our own houses.
- We don't want the sanitary napkins wrapped up in a newspaper.
- We don't want to skip the most awaited festivals.
- We don't want to be that unspoken scheduled gender.

Menstrual hygiene

Menstrual hygiene should be included in the basic requirements of life. The price in addition to the taxes of the sanitary napkins are ultimately high that makes it unaffordable for people below the poverty line. Women who couldn't afford to buy these products prefer using clothes. Some even can't afford clean cloth so they end up in dangerous practices like using soil and ashes packed underwear to soak up the blood. This will lead to a lot of health issues. Now, people are slowly getting awareness about this issue. Still there are women who don't even know the existence of products to help them during periods. They don't know what is meant by a sanitary napkin. This has to come to an end. It is our responsibility to create awareness and also donate to organisations that support women with menstrual hygiene. Hats off to those actions made in favour.

"Untouchability is a sin not only in the grounds of caste but also of gender. "

That one word 'second-hand' was enough to shatter all her trust in him. She was aghast in a way that her brain went numb and she started to cry. She was so traumatized, that she didn't even realize that he was tying her hands and legs to the bed. He raped her brutally and she denotes the pain occurred as unimaginable.

When she woke up the next day, he behaved as if nothing had happened. Jasmine convinced herself that it was normal.

She had left her job before the wedding as she was expected to be a loving housewife, who would cook and clean. So, she had to deal with the situation. She didn't want to be a two-time divorcee. But she got another blow- she found out that her husband was a drug addict. To his family, he was a perfect son, but behind the closed doors he would get high on crystal meth. He was so smart that he didn't indulge in alcohol since people would be able to smell it on him.

Jasmine was the only one subjected to his evil side.

CHAPTER VI

MARRIAGE vs CAREER

> *"Marriage can wait, education cannot. - Khaled Hosseini, <u>A thousand splendid suns.</u>"*

Although the law prescribes that the minimum age for marriage is 21 years for men, the Indian parents never urge their son to get married even at 25 or 26. The undetermined or perhaps, not-a-big-deal kind of criteria of marriage makes us feel jealousy. Because we women are often snaked by that nosy question of a far relative or an unfamiliar neighbour 'what's next?'

A man's life story consists of his career, his struggles, the way he tackled those struggles, his achievements and a lot more. A woman's life story also consists of all these elements but in most occasions, they are not of hers but of her husband's. Because, when a woman begins to dream of her career, simultaneously her parents dream of her marriage. They are not given the right of choices. *Marriage isn't a life-time goal.* It's just a part of life. However, most of the Indian parents want their daughters to be safe under the protection of her husband. If you think a woman is safe with her husband, think about marital rapes. She isn't safe anywhere. If you think an unmarried woman as unsafe, the problem is obviously in few men of the society. Forcing a woman to marry in her early ages is the same as telling a man that he is a threat to the safety of a woman.

Another reason for this crisis is few women itself. Women who have no aim in life other than their lifetime

33

goal of marriage, are the main essence of this problem to the fellow women those who want to live their life. Because these women let a picturisation of an ideal woman as the one who marries and takes care of her family all the time. By doing so, they let their fellow women down by promoting the concept of marriage. Again, I'm not against the concept of Marriage. I just wish for *a healthy system that doesn't force women into a married life.*

I would like to call the ambition- driven women the 'super-women' although society stamps them as 'bad-women'. I really don't understand why having an ambition in life is such a big crime. Anyway, I personally have a huge respect for these women. If you respect the feeling of a man, respect that of a woman's too. We aren't made of stone. We have dreams and the talent to achieve them. We should be given the right over our decision of if and when should we marry. We don't always want a man to buy something we want. Let us have a career of our own and live a lifestyle in which we buy them with the money we have earned.

I cannot help but wonder why no one will ever ask a man to choose between career and family. But this question has become usual to women. Here, another thing to notice is that men are denied the choice of selection between the two.

"A Career should not be an option for women and a compulsion for men. "

The honeymoon scenario was worse. She caught him having sex with someone else. She lost all the hope she had as the abuse continued. Meanwhile, he loved to see people in pain.

Jasmine lost weight and would always have bruises all over her body. Whenever she visited her parents, she would wear full-sleeves. Once, her sister saw a bruise on her neck and asked about it. But Jasmine lied saying that she had fallen. Her family thought she was happy. she was in a situation to present herself such.

All the while, he would keep on threatening to kill her, to chop her into pieces or even to fake her suicide. He had a clean image, so even if she told anyone, no one would believe her. She was terrified and began recording the abuse on her phone as evidence. She was afraid that what if she died and no one knew what really happened to her. She gave her cousin the password to her phone.

For three months, he tied her and raped her. She was very naive back then- because when she found out she was pregnant, she thought he would change. But she was wrong. When she told him about the pregnancy, he kicked her in the stomach. He didn't even let her cry out loud. He covered her mouth so that no one would hear her scream. she started bleeding and he had no choice other than taking her to the hospital.

They were on the way to hospital, when he made an attempt to kill her.

CHAPTER VII

GENDER STEREOTYPING

"I'm not the women president of Harvard. I'm the president of Harvard - Drew Gilpin Faust "

No one can predict the life of a child at the time of its birth. But we could surely say that the life story of this child definitely depends upon whether the child is a girl or a boy. Why is it so? The reason is that the life of a boy and a girl aren't the same. They are completely different stories. one of the reasons for this contrast is *gender stereotyping.*

Gender stereotyping is the preconception or generalization of a view on particular gender that may lead to limitations. Each and every human nature is precisely unique. We cannot simply have an overview of a set of characteristics on account of a person's gender. This will ultimately lead to inequality. Men are not an exception to this. They too face stereotypes and they eventually break them. A few men are unaware of this stereotyping that is slowly dragging them into darkness and putting them into serious mental stress. But gender stereotyping on a woman is obvious. It begins at the time of her birth itself.

When a man wants to succeed, he has to work hard whereas when a woman wants to succeed, she has to come across a huge mountain and each part of this mountain is made of gender stereotypes, condemnation and criticization. The peak of this mountain is Gender stereotyping. Men need not break stereotypes to achieve their goal whereas women have to. A man is praised for doing a thing whereas a woman is criticized and character assassinated*for doing the same.* This is when stereotyping invites inequality. This is especially when something is not supposed to be right.

Despite the fact that my parents brought up me and my brother with the same care, I could see a lot of differences in the opportunities we get. Thus, I came to understand that family alone is not the reason for such stereotyping. Society plays a major role.

It is easier to break the stereotypes than to make others accept it. Some are praised and the rest are despised for doing so. Let us have some fun by breaking a few here.

Alcoholism

I can't help but laugh at a man who hates women who drink alcohol despite the fact that he himself is an alcoholic. I'm against alcohol and believe that alcoholism is bad for health and the people around us regardless of gender. If you hate women who drink, hate men too. *Selective criticization is equally bad.* Show some equality be it appreciation or depreciation.

Education

Never choose your career based on your gender and never let anyone to. Never invite your gender into your capacity. Never limit a girl's education just to get her married to a man. Never reject her for her over-qualified educational degree than that of yours. Women are equally capable of studying any kind of stuff. Let her study and let her live on her own.

Restrictions

There are several restrictions that are brought into the path to happiness of a woman especially in religiously bound families. Meanwhile the man of the same family is provided with freedom. This is followed as an action taken towards the crimes that are happening against women. It would have been better if they had acted in opposition to the men who commit those crimes.

Have you ever thought why women are very self-conscious? The reason is that the restrictions the family and the society imposed on us, restricted our true selves. We just want to remove these unequally distributed restrictions without trace.

Love

A man's love with a woman is more easily accepted by the family of the man than that of a woman. There is no point in judging the value of a relationship with concern to gender. A disgusting fact is that a man is praised and even celebrated for having a girlfriend whereas a woman is *burnt alive* or emotionally blackmailed for doing the same.

Transsexual

Have you ever noticed that a transman is less susceptible to humiliation than a transwoman? This shows that femininity is used as a tool for humiliation. Women are welcomed with their tomboy appearance but men are offended just for wearing a pink shirt. *Femininity and masculinity cannot be limited in genders.* Go see a girl hitting a gym with toned biceps. At the same time, you can also see a man adorably flexible. It is inappropriate to judge someone for their way of carrying themselves.

Housecraft

Now-a-days, We women started to have a job of our own. Yet, the one thing that doesn't change is the women doing the same household chores along with the other tasks. The society piled this heavy stress on a woman saying that women are capable of multitasking. We are not and we don't want to. Let men do the equal household stuff. While I am asking for equality in house, we still have families in India that ask women to cook, serve and wait for the men of the family to get a complete meal and then they should eat. How absurd!

Crime

Women are celebrated in India which is a good thing actually. But there is a hurdle in disguise. When there is a public image of seeing women as divine, they are expected to be right all the time. You will ask me 'what's wrong in expecting the right thing from a person?'. I'll tell you. Expecting the right thing is fine. Here, the question is 'what is supposed to be the right thing?'.*There is a difference between what is right and what is supposed to be right.*

She knows to drive.
She prefers black to pink.
She watches cricket.
She hates gossiping.
She doesn't have long hair.
She reads crime novels.
She loves thriller movies.

She dresses up for her comfort.
She commits mistakes.
She is a pilot.
She is an astronaut.
She is a leader.
And she needs not prove it.

They were on his scooter on the way to hospital. Little did she expect, he threw her off, hoping she would get hit. Fortunately, she survived but instead of taking her to the hospital, he took her to his sister's house. There, his sister made him take her to the hospital. There, she called her mom. The doctor said Jasmine had an ectopic pregnancy & if she didn't have surgery immediately, she would die. Hearing this, her husband wasted 6 hours; he hoped she would bleed out and die. Jasmine's mom got suspicious & get the operation done—but Jasmine lost her baby.

The next day, he asked for a divorce. He said that she had disrespected his parents & that she refused to have sex with him, inspite of the fact that she was pregnant. He took advantage of her first marriage and made up this story. Jasmine finally told her mother the truth. She also told her she would go back to him, so that she could save her family from shame. But her mother stopped her from going back. Jasmine went to the police station to get an FIR filed even before she recovered from her trauma; but no one cared.

One day, she went to his house with her mother to get her gold & certificates back—but he kicked Jasmine's stomach & slapped her mom.

CHAPTER VIII

DOMESTIC VIOLENCE

"Nothing in the world was so bad as physical pain. In the face of pain there are no heroes. - George Orwell, 1984 "

A slap that has caused an eye to swell and the other to shed tears, a sudden push to the floor that you lose control, a scream at your face, an insult in front of others, a verbal abuse, a threatening to cause harm and even a raise of hand with an intention to hit you- all of these come under *domestic violence*. You may be under the control of an abusive husband or an overprotective parent. You may love them. At least, realize that what they are doing to you is no good for both your mental and physical health.

As a matter of fact, domestic violence is the most frequently occurring crime. Every third woman in India faces domestic violence either physically or sexually. It is absolutely a crime despite the relation between the people involved. Ask yourself - Have you ever seen your father or your relative hitting his wife? Have you ever seen a scene in a movie where a girl is being hit badly and verbally abused for falling in love? The answer will probably be yes. Ask yourself again - Have you ever seen a wife hitting her husband? Think again. You might have heard it as a joke.

Domestic Violence and Alcoholism

It has been a usual scenario in the rural regions of India for a drunk husband to harm his wife and children. I have seen several such incidents in my life. I have heard such an incident from a friend and a friend of a friend too. I have faced it myself too. But I refuse to stay quiet. That's what brought me here telling you that it isn't supposed to be so. Domestic violence is the main reason for people in our country to be against alcoholism. Do you think those men stay quiet after a drink? They don't.

Again, the family honours stop a woman from telling the world about her sufferings. She thinks it is better to stay silent and bear the pain rather than telling others and getting disappointment as a result. She is waiting for the society to get ready to listen to her. But when will that happen?

How to deal?

Realize the standard of your relationship. If you are being insulted and humiliated in front of others, if you are in agony, if you are in dissatisfaction, if your choices are being judged, you are in a toxic relationship. Taking the next step is up to you. You may not try to come out of your cage. At least realize, you are caged.

Select a happy relationship. Arranged marriages are the major sources of unhappy relationships. The choice is yours. You are the protagonist of your story. Neither your parents nor your sibling is going to travel along. Reduce the risk by doing it on your own, according to your own instincts.

Understand your partner. You should be aware of the dark side of your partner before getting into a serious relationship. Appearance does not matter in love but character does.

Mistakes happen. Sometimes it will be tricky. Your own choice may be wrong. There are few men out there who are masters in deception. Whatever it is, it is never too late. Call off your relationship if your partner seems to be abusive.

File a complaint. The protection of women from Domestic Violence Act ,2005 is at your service. Let your voice be heard but at the right forum.

Never be afraid of a failure. Divorce isn't a big deal. Especially If you have children, don't let them face it. Save them from being victimized. Let not your child face that unjust mental trauma. There is a life awaiting you. Come back and start again.

"*Realization is the first step. It is never too late.*"

Finally, the police took her statement. She waited for hours and he kept skipping court dates. There, she came to know about other Muslim women who were fighting similar cases for over 5 years. Jasmine was just 22. This is not what she wanted from life. She lost hope of justice. She realized that it would take too long for him to be sentenced, but she was capable of building a better future. She made a deal with her husband—she would withdraw her case if he returned her gold & certificates & signed the divorce papers. He agreed. she silenced her anger & moved on.

Jasmine wanted to go somewhere, where no one knew her. She wanted a peaceful life. But again, her family stood in her way. They wanted to keep her at home. To make sure she didn't leave India or get a job, they burned her passport & certificates.

CHAPTER IX

MASS MEDIA

"The representation of women in the society, especially through mass media has been the most delusional act ever done on the grounds of human existence. — Abhijit Naskar, <u>The Bengal Tigress: A Treatise on Gender Equality</u> "

Media plays an influential role in our everyday life. We can't simply deny the fact that the entertainment media has become a part of our life. It is an apt platform for making changes. But in certain cases, instead of making changes the media is emphasising the existence of stereotypes. It endows some superficial portrayals which may lead to a misunderstanding of the way of life itself. The way women are portrayed is something to be discussed. So, let us discuss.

Have you ever noticed that in Indian television serials, women play the lead role in most of the cases? Imagine a heroine of a serial. A fair, fit and young girl with long hair is doing chores to hold her family together and she enjoys serving her husband. Isn't it? In case, if the heroine is not fair, the whole story revolves around how she struggles and survives with a darker complexion. It should have been considered normal. *When a darker complexion is conceptualized, it definitely bothers.* If you portray it as a big deal, it will be a big deal. This applies to some movies too. They portray an image that is creating troubles. Changing the name of a fairness cream isn't sufficient. Let everyone know the reason behind it.

All of us might have come across this term called 'Homely girl'. 90% of Indian television dramas and serials have a tag of this term. I actually hate this word 'homely'. What in the world do you mean by a homely girl? The meaning is obvious. If you want to marry a girl who should do nothing but stay at home and do household chores, tell it directly. Don't create a favour for yourself in the name of women. It is clearly a clever patriarchy.

Long vs strong hair

Whenever the heroine has short hair, there will be a flashback that explains her transformation. If it had been considered normal, it won't bother a girl when she wants to chop her hair off. Not all girls want long hair. I wish I had short hair so that I don't need to spend hours taking care of it. But I can't do it. Why? The society won't be accepting it and so my mother. Men too had long hair. But they evolved with respect to their choice and comfort. It should have been normal for women too. But it is not.

Body hair

A body hair removal advertisement always shows a woman shaving her hairless body. Why is it so? Don't they want to capture an actual characteristic of the human race? I have rarely come across a picture showing the body hair of a woman. This shows the hesitation in showing the real nature of a human body. There is a business behind this which I don't want to explain here. Women too have body hair. Consider it as normal irrespective of whether a woman wishes to remove her body hair or not.

Villainism

Why do 90% of the movies have a man as a villain and not women? Here, men are portrayed as aggressive and strong to compete with and women as dignified at the same time powerless. Men too need their share of goodness. Some men are considered feminine only because of their incompetence. This should not be the case.

Sarcasm

Unrealistic fun shows always use a woman as their concept. Firstly, the hostess of the show is mocked during the whole time for her appearance and costume. I don't know why people are unaware that they are laughing at body shaming. Secondly, the men in the show would die laughing on a misogynistic joke. Thirdly, a man in women's attire is considered sarcastic but a woman in men's attire is not. The reason behind this unconscious disposition is that femininity is considered as something to be laughed at. I have come across a meme recently, where a young girl in a school uniform is being slapped inhumanly and there is a background music running behind making fun out of it. I felt very ashamed to be in a society where a crime is made fun of.

The role

In every single movie, when a woman is in trouble, there will be a man to rescue her. This is definitely being registered in the minds of the people watching. This will eventually lead to the idea of women being dependent.

Women will expect someone to protect her. This will end up in her anxiety during an actual trouble. And this anxiety is the trouble itself. Some movies give us no clue about the necessity of the heroine role. She will be there in the whole movie for no reason.

In the name of women-centred movies, some directors are glorifying the women on an unnecessary basis. when womanhood is glorified, there comes a lack of normality. We neither want movies that defocus nor that glorify women.

"We just need normalcy and impartiality. "

Jasmine didn't lose her spirits. She turned against her parents and filed a complaint against them in the Women's Cell for burning the documents. She tried everything—she told her mother she would publicly shame her & go to the media. Finally, they agreed to get new documents with a contract stating she had no right to the family property. Property was not in her mind. She readily agreed. For the first time in her life, she put her needs above theirs.

Jasmine left for Kochi with Rs.5000, stayed in a hostel & interviewed to be a receptionist at a fitness centre. She begged the owner for a chance, otherwise she would have to go back. He hired her; her salary was Rs.11,000; it was her first victory.

CHAPTER X

SYMPATHY? NO

"A gender-equal society would be one where the word 'gender' does not exist: where everyone can be themselves.— Gloria Steinem "

The governance of India has made a humpty of things in favour of women. Women are prioritized in several instances. A simple example is the seating arrangement in public transportation. *When there is a concept of prioritization, it should have come across a concept of equitation.* You have to equate something before you intend to raise its level. Priority is meaningless with the existence of inequality. You keep on increasing the height of a building while the basement itself is unstable. Equality is the basement. Meanwhile, Priority seems to be emphasizing the inferiority.

The subconscious weakness

Let us recall the events that happened during schooldays. Boys are punished severely but girls are forgiven with mild punishments. Are we that much weak to not bear the punishments for our own mistakes? Every woman might have heard this sentence once in a lifetime: 'I am forgiving you just because you are a girl. If you were a boy, I would not have treated you in the same way.' We need equality in everything regardless of its nature. Not only in offers but also in retribution.

Actually, this is the source. We are seeded and grown up with these thoughts subconsciously. This is when a woman considers herself inferior. prioritization and pampering also lead to this inferiority. We don't want us to be considered a weak, humble soul. This sympathising mentality leads to nothing but harassment. Here is where the shaming of periods initiates. Here is where an idea of rape initiates. And here is where the reason for the death of many innocent souls initiates. If your mentality is a reason for the loss of someone's life, why are you holding it?

The sympathy toward women is indeed painful when we have to struggle on a daily basis for equality. *There is inequality in perception. There is inequality in respect. There is inequality in importance. There is inequality in opportunity.* I have never seen a man sit on the floor in my entire lifetime and I am expected to sit on the floor just because I was born in this patriarchal society. I would rather stand. But for a good cause.

Women would never prioritize sympathy over equality. So, before prioritizing and sympathizing women, prioritize our priority.

> **"Sympathy or Empathy isn't the shit we thrive for.**
> **We aren't a hurt little wounded bird.**
> **WE ARE WOMEN**
> **"**

Jasmine discovered herself into fitness. She was just 35 kgs then. She gained weight by working out. She changed her entire look; she chopped off her hair. She no longer cared for men who love long hair. She found her true sexuality as a lesbian. She completed a course on fitness training. She is working as a trainer at a gym under the ownership of ex- Mr. India. She addresses it as once in a lifetime opportunity. She also believes that no matter how hard we try, we can't plan life.

Epilogue

The reason for including the tale of Jasmine is to portray the reality of life for an Indian woman. She has faced domestic violence, marital rape, society's disgrace and a lot more. The worst part is that, even today, she is getting rape threats for talking against a religion. But she is valorous and an inspiration to many. She won't step back. The trauma in her life was so painful that these nuisances won't harm her anymore. Thanks to Jasmine M Moosa for giving me an opportunity to tell her tale.

For all the miseries, sufferings, rapes, abuses, violence, stereotypes and disgrace, we only expect two things- *justice and equality.*

Thanks for your patience. The thing you hold in your hand right now is not of a single voice but of a thousand. If I could change the perception of a single person through this book, I have achieved my goal.

A Note From A Friend About The Author

Hi folks. Hope you all are doing good. I am glad to introduce myself as a good friend of the author. It has been many years of beautiful friendship since our kindergarten together and the essence of it still stays the same. It is something to be wondered that she keeps on showing constant love. Isn't it an unexpected blessing to have a friend who holds our hands throughout all the stages of our life? She is the one to be loved for various qualities. She is a rare one who lightens up others like a dazzling lamp even during her own hard times.

Being an avid reader, she has added writing to the list of several things she does. She is a fearless lioness with a greater courage within, who raises her voice wisely. Somewhere, I am being inspired by her vivacious and socialistic thoughts. Every time, she makes me wonder how could one be such an all-rounder. Only her determination brought her all this way. This classy girl deserves to shine brighter and fly higher. She has a long way to cherish and this journey is absolutely going to be awesome.

Best wishes to the gem!